I0030752

Websites That Work

# WEBSITES THAT
# WORK:
## 10 LOW-COST, HIGH-ROI INTERNET MARKETING STRATEGIES

# PAUL J. SCOTT

© 2016 Paul J. Scott. All rights reserved. Printed and bound in the United States of America. No part of this book may be reproduced or transmitted in any form or by any means, electronic or mechanical, including photocopying, recording, or by an information storage and retrieval system – except by a reviewer who may quote brief passages in a review to be printed in a magazine, newspaper, or on the web – without permission in writing from the author.

*Cover & Book Design by Nikki Ward, Morrison Alley Design*

Although the author and publisher have made every effort to ensure the accuracy and completeness of information contained in this book, we assume no responsibility for errors, inaccuracies, omissions, or any inconsistency herein. Any slights of people, places, or organizations are unintentional.

First Printing 2016

ISBN 978-0-9966874-3-0

# Table of Contents

Introduction                                                        i

1   Build A Beautiful And Functional Website                        1

2   Get To Know Your Best Customers                                 17

3   Understand The New World Of SEO                                 33

4   Use Highly Targeted Search Engine Marketing                     49

5   Target Local Buyers Online                                      63

6   Use Social Media To Build Buzz                                  75

7   Your Email List Is Digital Gold                                 93

8   Build And Grow A Great Online Reputation                        107

9   Wash, Rinse, Repeat: Regularly Review
    Strategy And Analytics                                          121

10  Find The Right Web Design And
    Internet Marketing Partner                                      135

    Conclusion: The Secret Sauce Isn't So Secret                    149

    About The Author                                                157

# Introduction

## Introduction: Can You Really Succeed Online Without Spending A Fortune?

We live in an interesting age. The growth of the Internet, and an explosion in mobile technology, has brought us to a point where the web is almost *everywhere*, literally and figuratively. Tens of millions of people now walk around carrying smartphones and tablets, keeping the bulk of human knowledge in their pockets at any given moment.

That simple fact has changed the way business people think and operate. There are endless surveys and statistics that show how being Internet savvy has become crucial to running a successful company, but you don't need a lot of numbers to recognize the truth because it's all around us. On a recent reality TV competition, one of the competitors attributed the success of his food truck to a "comprehensive social media campaign."

In other words, a person selling hamburgers for cash, in a face-to-face setting, was relying on Facebook and Twitter to generate sales opportunities. Doesn't that just sum things up perfectly?

A lot of business owners lament that online marketing and social media have gotten to be too important. Some of them, usually men and women who've been in business for a long time, miss the days when a good print advertising campaign was enough; others hate that finding customers online seems to take so much time and money.

These are all valid concerns, but they miss the bigger point: *The Internet is a big democracy.* You don't have to be the biggest business to get the biggest results, and in fact you can often "take down" a much bigger and better-funded competitor with a little bit of insight and creativity.

Granted, it doesn't always seem this way. A lot of businesses get locked into the notion of spending a fortune to compete online, only to find that their hard-earned dollars aren't getting them the kinds of returns they'd hoped for. Some invest huge amounts of cash into modern websites with lots of features, but can't attract visitors (or turn those visitors into customers).

When these kinds of failures occur, one of two things usually happens. Some marketers will essentially double down on their mistakes, spending more and more money to chase the results they're looking for. If that doesn't work, or if the business doesn't have that kind of money to throw around in the first place, then a lot of owners and managers find themselves looking for the one "secret" that's going to unlock the key to huge profits.

The bad news is that this kind of secret doesn't exist – there usually isn't a simple adjustment you can make that will bring thousands of new customers to your doorstep overnight. The good news, however, is that there is a system that *will* give you those results, if you're willing to persevere and stick with it over time.

That system, which is more like a set of principles to follow, is going to be the topic of this book.

Just to be clear from the outset, what I'm promising you isn't a quick-fix, or an instant path to hidden riches. There aren't a lot of secrets found in the coming chapters. What you *will* read is a collection of commonsense best practices, gained from years of experience helping business owners and executives (*in other words, people just like you*) make meaningful improvements in their online marketing and offline profits.

Best of all, it's a set of guidelines you can follow again and again, even if you don't have a small fortune, or even several hours a day, to spend on Internet marketing. This is a guide for working people who need real-world answers. There is still going to be some cost and commitment required, but probably not as much as you might think. You don't have to break the bank or drive yourself crazy to find customers online, and you don't have to become an expert in websites or HTML code, either.

In just a moment, I'm going to start guiding you through ten key areas of Internet marketing to focus on. This book has been purposely divided into ten short sections that offer stand-alone topics, but work best together in conjunction with one another. With that in mind, I invite you to take a couple of hours and read through it once to get a sense of the overall philosophy. Then you can come back later and refer to individual chapters or sections as needed.

However you do it, though, I hope you'll take the time to implement the lessons that are coming into your daily business. Being successful on the web, and turning that success into real-world bottom-line improvement, is all about having the right approach and mindset to specific marketing activities. Make these habits and ideas your own, and you'll be well on the way to building something extraordinary.

With all of that out of the way, it's time to get to work. Let's see how the smartest companies succeed in Internet marketing while adhering to reasonable budgets.

# 1 | Build A Beautiful And Functional Website

It's easier than ever to get a website for your business. That's not always good news, though, because it means anyone can launch one... and that it's harder than ever to make your business stand out online.

If your website looks like every other website – or at least every other website in your business or industry – then you're going to have a hard time making a good first impression on visitors. Those first impressions might matter more than you think.

Going back just a few decades, when a lot more business was being conducted face-to-face, or over the phone, a business with a great product, low pricing, or a convenient location could get away with a few deficiencies in their marketing. Because a customer might know and like the owner, or not have many other choices, they would be more willing to take the chance, even if they weren't blown away by things like advertisements.

In the digital age, we have a situation that's almost the opposite. A lot of customers will look up the business online before they ever buy anything, *even if it's a retail location down the street.* That's a topic and theme we'll return to when it's time to look at your online reputation, but the immediate point to be made is that your website *has* to make the right first impression on customers.

Let's take a look at some of the ways you can ensure that it will…

## Find A Domain Name That Makes Sense

Unless your business is a startup, there is a great chance you already have a website with its own domain name. You might even have one you've used for years.

Even so, it's worth bringing up the value of domains here because too many businesses settle for "online real estate" that is hard to spell, hard to remember, or doesn't really reflect anything about the company itself. Over the long run, these kinds of mistakes can negatively impact your Internet marketing campaigns in important ways.

The best domain names are short, intuitive, and free of dashes or hyphens. If you are considering revamping your approach to Internet marketing, start by evaluating the space where your website actually lives and make sure you have a domain name that makes sense for your business.

## *Choose A Layout That Accomplishes Three Things*

Web design can be deceptively complex. On the one hand, you'll have noticed that most websites follow a very similar format, especially on the homepage. The graphics and text might change, but most have a fairly uniform look.

That's not an accident. As it turns out, your layout has to accomplish a lot of different things all at the same time. In order to leave the right first impression on visitors, it should make you seem like a credible and professional business, make it clear to a first-time visitor exactly who you are and what you do, and give a few options to take further action.

If your website doesn't accomplish those tasks, then it's not doing its job (and the lack of results is going to cost you money). If you don't seem professional, people won't trust you enough, or take you seriously enough, to hang around on your website. If what your business is about seems unclear, they may not stick around long enough to find the answers. And if there aren't some clear follow-up steps, then you're counting on the fact that potential customers are going to pick up the phone or visit you in person, not to mention that they'll do so before they forget, get distracted, or find one of your competitors.

For that reason, your website must have a layout that accomplishes those three objectives. It's fine to experiment and be unconventional, but don't lose sight of what's important.

## Focus On Clean Design And Great Usability

This ties onto the last point, but it's important enough to mention on its own. When people outside the web design and marketing industry think about "good" websites, they often have trouble qualifying exactly what they think. Some people prefer certain colors and fonts over others, but most of us can agree whether a particular layout looks "professional" or not even if we can't say why.

That's *why*, more often than not, it comes down to clean design: pages that are easy to understand and have lots of white space.

As humans, we tend to find clutter distracting. That's especially true on the web, where lots of things seem to be flashing and crying out for attention all at the same time. A clean design makes it easy for us to organize and process the information found on a page, and causes less subconscious stress than something that's busier.

Along with clean design you should consider its twin, usability. You've probably heard that term, but might not be familiar with its exact meaning. In this context, usability simply refers to the ease with which your website visitors can make their way from one topic or idea to the next. In other words, it's all about how quick and simple it is for them to find the information they are looking for.

When usability is maximized, a website feels straightforward and intuitive. When menus, navigations, and search bars aren't easy to find and use, the same pages feel like frustrating dead ends.

Most customers will never talk to you about clean design and usability, or even notice it consciously, but they definitely feel the difference when they're using your pages. And that can be the difference between having them stick around your website or take their business elsewhere.

## *Use Visuals That Are Memorable For The Right Reasons*

As great as a strong web layout is, people tend to not notice the structure of your pages in a direct way. Instead, they may have a notion of whether they like using your website or not, but without firm reasons why.

One thing they *will* certainly key in on, though, are the visuals you use on your pages. Specifically, I'm talking about photographs, logos, and illustrations.

Photographs, in particular, are very important to your web design. Studies have shown that the human mind can process an image hundreds of times faster than it can a line of text. That means that photographs make an instant and emotional connection with a web visitor that headlines and blocks of body copy can't.

Knowing that, the decision to fill a website with stock photos can be a costly convenience. Certainly, these kinds of images have their place, and can be a quick and convenient solution to filling in a company's webpages. A better option, though, is to populate a website with custom photographs showing the staff, the location, and the company's products. These make a stronger impression and can't be duplicated by competitors. Additionally, these custom photos can do double-duty in social media marketing, blog posts, and even employee profiles.

You'll recall that in the introduction I mentioned that you don't have to spend a fortune to succeed with Internet marketing, and that is certainly the case here. Getting custom photos doesn't have to cost a lot, and you can even work with a student or a part-time photographer to get the images you need. But it's worth making this small investment, instead of simply choosing stock photos, because the long-term return on investment could be significant.

## Don't Settle For A Non-Responsive Website

Although Internet marketing strategies and concepts are more important than specific technical details, there is one that deserves special mention here: *responsive web design.*

At the time of this writing, more than half of all web traffic is coming through mobile devices like smartphones and tablets. That percentage is rising every single day, and it won't surprise anyone if mobile traffic eventually makes up three quarters or more of your website visitors.

Mobile web functionality, once a sub-topic of Internet marketing, has gone mainstream. You simply can't compete online these days without having a mobile-friendly web presence, and that usually means getting a responsive website that adapts itself to different screen sizes and platforms.

Mobile visitors are simply too important to your business to ignore, so don't bury your head in the sand and assume that your website is perfectly functional even though it was designed for desktop computers seven or eight years ago. If you aren't up to date with a responsive layout, take steps to fix that problem *today*. If you don't, it's going to keep costing you more and more until it's too late.

## Pay Close Attention To Your Grammar and Messaging

It's a strange thing, but business owners and managers tend to love thinking about web designs and layouts, but hate dealing with online copywriting. That makes sense in that visuals are usually more fun than text, but it's just not good business.

No matter how impressive your website looks, the text on your pages is what's going to ultimately interest visitors and sell your products and services. At a minimum, that means it has to be coherent and grammatically up to snuff. Ideally, you'll want something that's interesting, unique, and persuasive.

To get that kind of writing on your website, you'll probably have two options. The first is to spend a lot of hours putting words on screens yourself. While this might carry all the excitement of a ninth-grade research paper, it can sometimes be the very best way to get the web content you need. After all, nobody knows your business as well as you do, and no one has as much passion or insight about your customers and products.

At the same time, most business people don't enjoy writing, aren't particularly great at it, and wouldn't have the time to work on their webpages even if they were. For those reasons, working with a professional copywriter who can take your ideas and turn them into persuasive paragraphs and bullet points can make a lot of sense.

You might have missed it, but the key word in that last paragraph was "professional." There are a lot of people calling themselves writers, and happy to take your money, even though they don't have any more skill or experience than you do. Even worse, some of them are going to ship your project overseas, to a "copywriter" who learned English as a third or fourth language.

Remember that the content on your website has to build up your credibility and convince buyers to take the next step, whether that's to buy a product, visit your store, sign up for an email newsletter, or do something else. Don't hire someone you aren't sure is up to the task.

## Pay Close Attention To Your Grammar And Messaging

It's a strange thing, but business owners and managers tend to *love* thinking about web designs and layouts, but hate dealing with online copywriting. That makes sense in that visuals are usually more fun than text, but it's just not good business.

No matter how impressive your website looks, the text on your pages is what's going to ultimately interest visitors and sell your products and services. At a minimum, that means it has to be coherent and grammatically up to snuff. Ideally, you'll want something that's interesting, unique, and persuasive.

One more note to add here is that working with a writer or editor doesn't have to be an all-or-nothing proposition. You may want to start your web content by putting down a few notes and thoughts on each page, and then meet with someone (in person or over the phone) who can turn your ideas into marketing gold. Doing so takes a little more time than just handing the project off to someone else, but it can be a great way to ensure that your most important marketing messages come through.

As with custom images, getting professional content for your website is one of those things where you spend pennies now to save dollars later. It can be tempting to skip the investment in good writing, whether it's in time or money, but you'll end up regretting it later.

## Make Sure Your Website Has A Point

It's amazing how many business owners will pour time and money into a new website simply because they feel sure that they "need one." They aren't necessarily wrong, but what do you actually need your website for?

What I'm driving at here is the idea that your website should have a point. There should be a set of specific business goals that you're trying to meet by launching it, and knowing what those goals are now will help you immensely later.

For example, the point of your website might be to drive online sales. Or, it could be to help inform current and potential customers about sales, specials, and in-store events. The point could also be to assist with recruiting and customer service. In fact, it's probably some combination of all of these things.

When you know the point of your website, it's easier to design, write, and revise your pages. And it's a lot simpler to visualize successful campaigns in the future if you know what you're aiming at. Your website should have a point, and you'll want to find that point before you get started with anything that involves "knocking down walls" by designing new pages or removing elements that are already online.

One way to help find the point of your website, and to improve your Internet marketing campaigns in general, is to think more closely about who your site really needs to appeal to. That's something we are going to explore more closely in the next section.

# 2 | Get To Know Your Best Customers

At about the same time that Internet marketing started to be such a big deal, business owners began to pick up on a notion that anyone, anywhere could be a potential customer. Unfortunately, that's just not true. Although the Internet allows you to reach anyone, the reality is that most people still aren't going to be in the market for what you have to sell or offer.

That's not to say that things aren't different, though. For one thing, the web makes it easier to reach potential buyers who are in your immediate geographic area (although many of your best customers still might come from down the street, something we'll explore later). And for another, it has made marketing more specific.

To understand why, we only have to look at things from the point of view of our customers. That's not difficult, since we are all buyers as much as we are sellers. Before the Internet, you essentially had a few different choices for buying, whether you were thinking about consumer products or business-to-business purchases. You could visit a local retailer (or dealer), order something from a catalog, or find a vendor who could get you exactly what you wanted... and probably spend a lot of time or money in the process.

Now, as we all know, the information, products, and services we are looking for can be found right at our fingertips. We don't have to go through any of these complicated buying channels because we can find the *exact* item or solution we want and need online, often in a matter of seconds. In fact, we can probably comparison-shop to see where it's available, who has the lowest price and the fastest shipping, and which suppliers offer the best terms or have the highest reviews.

When we reverse roles again, it's easy to see why we have to put ourselves in our customers' shoes. They have a lot of choices, and they're looking for the *exact* answer for their needs. If you aren't providing it, someone else will be.

So within your market as a whole there are lots of smaller niches. Almost everyone in the world might be a potential sandwich-buyer, for example, but a much, much smaller slice of that population is going to be interested in Italian-style subs, sold in Chicago, featuring all local ingredients. Or, you could say that nearly every business needs printing at some point or another, but only a fraction of them need commercial print-on-demand services with full-color functionality and next-day delivery in New Jersey.

We could go on and on with these kinds of theoretical examples, but you probably get the idea. Unless you're selling something like Coca-Cola or Pepsi, most of the world isn't a great prospect for what you want to sell – even though you can theoretically reach them – and trying to market to everyone would be a huge waste of time and money.

So, while Internet marketing is making your pool of buyers bigger, it's also making them smaller and more specific at the same time. Your best potential customers, the ones who will buy from you again and again, write positive reviews about your company, and pay the most for your products or services, all probably have a few traits in common.

Let's take a closer look at what those traits might be, and the tools you can use to find them…

## Who Are Your Perfect Customers?

Although your perfect customers likely have some things in common, what those things are will depend a great deal on your industry and the specifics of your company. Let's look at some of the most common ways to group buyers and find out who your most important customers and prospects might be.

*Interest or Need* – Let's begin with the obvious. Some people are good potential customers for what you offer (and some aren't), simply based on their individual needs and interests. The person who is interested in a sports car might not be in the market for a minivan; someone shopping for crutches isn't probably looking to buy rollerblades, too.

These distinctions are fairly obvious, but you can take this concept to a deeper level to think about what *really* interests the men and women who are going to buy from you. And don't forget that this kind of thinking also applies to business-to-business marketing situations. Only some people are going to even consider buying what you sell.

*Geography* – For some kinds of businesses, geography can also be an obvious qualifier. Maybe people only tend to buy from you when they live in the same neighborhood, or are passing through. Or perhaps you have restrictions on shipping, advertising, or legal guidelines that make it cost-prohibitive for you to do business elsewhere.

As with needs and interests, this might seem obvious. But if you have geographical constraints, it's important to think about them carefully, and to determine how firmly they apply to you and your customers.

*Knowledge Level* – Do you tend to attract customers who are very well-informed about your business, or those who are new to your products or services? Do you have sophisticated buyers, or novices?

Determining the knowledge level of your most important buyers is critical, because it shapes the way you create web content and marketing messages. Go too low, and your perfect buyers might not take you seriously. Aim too high, and you could miss out on those who need more of an introduction.

*Buying Motivations* – Why are your potential customers choosing to buy at all? The more you know about their real motivations, the easier it is for you to tailor your approach in a way that works for them.

As an example, a hairstylist might say that her clients "want to look good." That's an easy conclusion to draw, and it's a good start. But *why* do they want to look good? If she knows, for example, that customers tend to see her before a big job interview, or a wedding, then that would certainly change the dynamic a bit and affect her marketing.

*Price Sensitivity* – Some people are willing to pay whatever it takes to get the best. Others will cut corners endlessly until they feel like they've gotten a rock-bottom deal. And some buyers will fall into both categories, just depending on how strongly they feel about the purchase, and whether they have an emotional attachment to it.

You need to know what your customers respond to within your market. Are they price-sensitive, and doing business with you because you offer the biggest discounts, or do they want quality and service no matter what they see on the price tag or invoice? It's very difficult to market your company to both types of buyers, so it's critical that you know where your most important customers place their priorities.

*Timing and Delivery Needs* – Pizzas aren't the only things that people want to see delivered quickly. If you can deliver a product, or finish with the service, faster than anyone else, that might be a big competitive advantage.

As with pricing, though, there are different types of buyers and preferences to consider. Some people want speed and are willing to pay for it. But other customers might want the best work they can afford, even if it takes a little longer. And of course, some customers will fall in the range between these two extremes.

Your job, as a business owner or manager, is to figure out which groups of buyers are most interested in what you have to sell, and which of these priorities matters the most to them.

*Personal Preferences* – This is a broad category, and one that is greatly dependent on the type of business you operate. There are thousands of different personal preferences that affect the way we buy things: foreign or domestic, light or dark, thin or deep dish, and so on.

Within your business, there are lots of things that distinguish you from your competitors. Without an awareness of what these are, and how they impact customer decisions, you can't market yourself as effectively as you should be.

## Look For Common Demographics

The deeper you get into thinking about who your best customers might be, the more likely you are to stumble across some demographic similarities. For example, maybe your most important customers are predominantly one sex or ethnicity, all live in the same few neighborhoods, or fall into a certain age range.

That kind of information can be helpful, because marketing by demographic is a relatively simple matter online. They are going to be some things about your best customers that you just can't quantify into a number or statistic, and that's fine. Those are things that will come through in your design, copywriting, and ongoing messaging.

The simple factors that you *can* identify, however, can form the basis for pay-per-click and social media campaigns (as examples). Modern web marketing technology makes it easy for you to zero in on a certain kind of person, so if you notice demographic trends developing for your business, make notes so you can take advantage of them later.

Note that you might not have to look very hard to find them. That's because basic analytics software (which we'll explore later) can give you a wealth of information about who is coming to your website and what they are looking at once they arrive. This isn't the same as having exact information like ages, addresses, and so on, but it puts a wealth of basic data right at your fingertips.

## *Building Buyer Profiles*

What you are really trying to accomplish with all of this is finding out more about the men and women who actually keep you in business. But while we have been discussing them as a distinct group so far, it's likely that you'll have at least two or three different types of buyers that matter.

That's okay. What I would encourage you to do is build a short "profile" for each one, encompassing all the kinds of information we have examined up to this point. One group might be older men with a certain set of preferences, while another could be young mothers who are making their decision based on entirely different criteria.

In many cases, you'll be able to tailor your marketing so that each group sees the messaging that's right for them. And for more general pieces (like your website), you can use language that appeals to all of your most important buyer profiles.

What you *don't* want to do, however, is try to make your online marketing campaigns work for everyone. The farther you get from your core audience, the closer you get to generic marketing mush that isn't meaningful to buyers at all. In other words, your first priority is to appeal to that group of potential customers who are the very best possible fit for what you have to offer. They are the ones who are going to spend the most and return to you time and time again.

That's not to say that your marketing can't work for others, or that no one else will buy from you. It's just the simple recognition that customers outside of your core profiles are likely to be less profitable, less satisfied, and more susceptible to your competitors. They aren't the ones who will help your business thrive in the long term, so it never makes sense to do something your best buyers wouldn't like just to earn a few more of their dollars in the short term.

## *Using What You Know To Improve Your Website And Marketing*

Going through all of this effort to find out who your most important buyers and prospects are can be tedious, but it's worth it. At a certain point, you'll begin to know your best customers as if they were real people. They *are* real people, of course, but what I mean is that you'll be able to take broad types of buyers and think about them in individual terms.

When that happens, you are well on the way to building a highly successful Internet marketing campaign. That's because you don't just know whom you're marketing to, but what they need and care about. You have a good idea of what their motivations and decision factors are like, so you can "push the right buttons" with your webpages, blog posts, emails, and pay-per-click ads.

When you know your customers, you can fine-tune even the smallest details to fit your audience. Decisions about things like design preferences, font size, and whether or not to emphasize pricing discounts in your marketing all become clear because you have a firm picture of your target in mind.

Far, far too many businesses try to market their products and services to generic customers that they don't really know anything about. But how can you put together effective messaging when you don't really know whom it's aimed at, or what that person wants from you?

Learning about your customers is the key that opens up everything else in your Internet marketing campaign, not to mention the rest of this book. So find out who your most important buyers are, and then keep learning as much as you can about them, remembering that profiles and demographics might change over time.

When businesses go out of business, it's often because their customers changed and they didn't adapt. But when they succeed year after year, it's usually because they kept on giving their very best customers exactly what they wanted.

# 3 | Understand The New
# World Of SEO

When you want to find out about something, where's the first place you turn for information? Unless there happens to be an expert on the subject standing just a few feet away, you probably do what most of us do and ask Google.

The world's largest search engine has become so ubiquitous that it handles somewhere around 2 billion different search queries *every single day*. About half as many go toward Bing, Yahoo, and other search tools.

Given the scale of those figures, it's probably not surprising that a lot of business people consider search engine optimization, which is the art and science of making your website appear more prominently in search engine listings, as being more or less the same thing as Internet marketing.

What people who hold on to this assumption don't usually realize is that they are missing two key details: First, there's more to finding customers than simply coming in first on Google; and second, what they think of as "search engine optimization" (or SEO) is probably outdated.

In this chapter we are going to take a look at why, and what you can do about it to give your business an advantage...

## *The Old World Of SEO*

When Google first came into the world, and search engines were still growing up, attracting visitors to your website was a relatively simple matter. It was known that search engines use "spiders," which are just automated pieces of software that look at the content of your website, and that these spiders would look for certain words and phrases that came up again and again in user searches. They would also look at links pointing from one website to another, treating any search terms they found within those links in the same way.

This simplistic model actually worked pretty well. Most of the time, searchers could find what they were looking for using a few terms and phrases.

Marketers caught on, of course, and early search engine optimization was incredibly straightforward. Once you knew what the key search terms for your business were, you could add these terms to your web content (even dozens or hundreds of times) and the search spiders would understand what your pages were about and send visitors to you.

However, the success of early SEO created its own problems. Soon, everyone was optimizing their websites, and some companies were optimizing for terms that didn't really apply to their businesses. As a result of search engine optimization becoming widespread, it was actually getting *harder* for searchers to find what they were looking for.

So, the engineers at Google and the other search engines started looking for other factors they could use to determine things like topic and relevance. They began paying attention to domain names, the age of the website, natural phrasing, citations, and the quality of a link coming from another website.

In other words, Google started separating positive search indicators from negative ones. And where it found too many problem areas, it started punishing marketers who were trying to abuse the system.

This final point is a very important one, because there are a lot of marketers (and truth be told, more than a few web designers and SEO "experts") who are still clinging to old ideas about the best ways to attract traffic to a website. Because they had some limited success with keyword stuffing and cheap links in the past, they continue holding out hope that they will continue to work in the future.

Hiring someone who holds on to these notions is worse than throwing away your money, because the more they do for you, the more invisible you are likely to become on Google and the other major search engines over time.

## The Rise Of Contextual Search

With subsequent changes to its search algorithm instituted over time, Google has embraced more of a natural, contextual approach to determining search results. That doesn't just mean that it goes beyond strictly matching keywords with search phrases, but also that other deeper factors are now considered.

For example, a few years ago Google engineers noticed that roughly one out of every five search strings contained a geographic element. In a short period of time, they were able to determine that searchers were looking for local businesses on the Internet, trying to find more up-to-date information than they would've gotten from the Yellow Pages and other print directories. As a result, the search algorithm was amended to prioritize local results over distant ones.

Similarly, the concept of authority and trustworthiness has become a central factor in search engine optimization. Google knows that results from older websites tend to be more reliable than newer ones (assuming that the website has been kept up to date), and that one with thousands of lengthy and unique pages is likely to be a better resource than a website with just a few short blurbs. And so, more authoritative search results are prioritized while "thin air" web destinations are largely ignored.

Another SEO innovation has been a change in the way that links are seen by search spiders. While any link could be considered a positive vote of confidence in the past, now low-quality links, or those coming from unrelated websites, are ignored or may actually harm your search visibility. Conversely, links coming from reputable websites with a high Google Page Rank (that is, websites with lots of visitors, engagement, and original content) are worth more than ever.

Even searcher behavior has been incorporated into the mix, both individually and across the web. For example, if Google sees that numerous users have clicked through to a website and then immediately left, that's taken as a sign that the destination isn't a great one. But, if people spend a lot of time looking at your website, clicking on links, and generally finding what they're looking for, then that's a cue that the website in question is a good resource.

On a more personal level, Google doesn't just match geography, but when it can it will take things like search history and context into account to try to determine searcher *intent*. This means that, based on the specific situation, a searcher can be directed toward several results pages that don't even have the same keywords, if Google thinks they are better results than can be found elsewhere.

To some marketers, and especially those holding on to old ideas about keywords and links, these changes can be incredibly frustrating. For users, however, they mean better results and less hassle.

Never forget that most people don't jump on the Internet thinking "I want to buy something!" Instead, they turn to Google and the other search engines because they have a question they want answered, or a problem they want solved. They may well decide to purchase something, or contact the company, as a result of that search for answers, but it usually isn't their first intention. So, the more your website is a resource for information and answers, the more popular it's likely to be with Google and the other search engines.

## The Long Tail Of Search Strings

The last few years have seen Google get pickier about its search results – actual users are demanding more relevant, specific, and timely destinations, as well. One of the ways we can tell is through the increase in so-called "long-tail" search strings.

In simple terms, long-tail search strings (named for the long tail of bell curve distributions) are search phrases that are highly specific and don't generate a lot of traffic on their own. Often, they build upon more common keywords and search terms. For example, while lots of people might search "Chicago web design," a long-tail version of that search string could be "Chicago web design for engineering firms."

There are two interesting things to note about long-tail search trends. The first is that even though these phrases don't get much traffic individually, they do *collectively* make up a big share of search traffic. Some estimates are that 20 to 30% of all search queries involve long-tail searches. In fact, roughly one out of every dozen strings entered into Google is completely original, meaning that it has never been searched before.

Knowing that so many search terms are unique and unusual, the second faction might be a big surprise: It's difficult to target long-tail searchers directly. In other words, if you were to try to use old-school SEO tactics, you would have to brainstorm thousands upon thousands of possible search terms, creating pages optimized for each one.

That's not feasible for any organization, much less a small or medium-sized business that's trying to maximize their return on investment of time and capital. But that doesn't mean you should give up on long-tail searchers altogether. Instead, you should embrace the new wave of contextual search and let Google do its job.

The more content you have on your website (and the more your pages are related to one another in terms of topic and tone), the easier it is for Google and the other search engines to understand what your website is "about." So, by adding lots of pages, and especially blog posts that are relevant to your industry, you can signal to Google that you are a great resource. Then they can easily match you with long-tail searchers, even if the exact search strings in question aren't found on your pages.

Of course, having lots of relevant content helps you with traditional search engine optimization as well. What's important to note here, however, is that when you attract long-tail searchers to your website, you're usually doing so with little or no competition. And, as it turns out, sometimes the most precise keywords end up being the most profitable ones, even if they aren't used as often...

## Keyword Research For Conversions, Not Visits

Traditionally, keyword research for search engine optimization goes something like this: A researcher looks up keywords and search terms related to a business that get lots of traffic, and puts them into a spreadsheet. Then, the business (or the web design firm helping out) targets those keywords by creating new pages, blog posts, social articles, etc.

The problem with this approach is that it assumes "traffic = sales." And I can tell you from experience that this kind of math is fuzzy, at best.

To be sure, you *do* need visitors to your website if you're going to generate leads and sales online. However, it's much more important to have the right visitors than it is to have lots of them. In fact, chasing the most heavily trafficked search terms can be an exercise in futility.

To see why, first consider that the vast majority of marketers are following the formula I outlined above. That means that the more traffic there is for a search term, the more businesses there are trying to optimize their websites for the keyword or phrase in question.

Then, think about the way you search yourself when you go online. Most people start with a broad set of search terms (those heavily trafficked keywords we just mentioned), and then refine their search terms down farther once they have found a bit of information and figured out what they were actually searching for in terms of products, information, etc.

That means that, in many cases, those initial searches using broad keywords aren't being performed by people who know what they need or intend to make a purchase. Why focus on those prospects when you could target the ones using longer, more precise search strings who are more serious about taking the next step, especially when doing so would let you bypass the competition?

Using basic and heavily search phrases as a starting point for your keyword research and SEO campaigns is a reasonable thing to do. But as you brainstorm ideas and compare options, remember that conversions matter more than visits and focus your energies appropriately.

The easiest way to increase the return you get from search engine optimization is to target more specific keywords. That allows you to get to the top of the search engine listings faster, and to generate more leads or sales from your campaigns. It's about working smart instead of pouring lots of money into the problem. If you want to achieve extraordinary results without breaking your budget, you can't afford to follow the same roadmap as every one of your competitors.

## Achieving A Light Touch With SEO

Perhaps the one thing you should really take away from the new reality of SEO is that it's much more subtle than it was in the past. In other words, you need to use a light touch.

It used to be the case that achieving a good search engine rank was all about cramming keywords in page titles and headings, and maybe having a few links point at your website for good measure. Now though, those kinds of tactics won't help you. In fact, they would serve as a signal to Google that you're trying to game the system and could result in your website not being displayed in the search engine listings at all.

Remember that searchers and search engines alike want natural, unique, and informative content. Your webpages and blog posts *should* have important search phrases, but you can use them sparingly and get a much bigger effect than you would by overloading visitors with odd-sounding sentences designed to be scanned by search spiders.

You want your website to be visible, on Google and elsewhere, but your bigger goal should be to impress visitors and earn new customers. Keywords and links are only a very small part of that equation. Jump into the new world of SEO by optimizing every page for sales, not drowning readers in search terms.

# 4 | Use Highly Targeted Search Engine Marketing

If you want to make the most of Google and the other search engines when it comes to attracting new customers to your website, then you should consider search engine marketing in addition to SEO.

In case you're not familiar with the difference, search engine marketing (also sometimes referred to as search marketing or SEM) has to do with placing paid ads on search engine listings. These often involve bidding a certain price for each click, but can also be based on impressions (the number of times an ad is seen) or overall conversions. They can also be simple text ads, image ads, or some combination of repeating ads (also known as retargeting) that are shown to prospects again and again.

The same model that you use for search engine advertising can even be carried over into social media. While that's not *technically* the same thing as search marketing, many of the same concepts come into play.

To keep things simple, and to keep the focus on the important principles of search marketing instead of minor details, we are going to lump them all together in this chapter. To be sure, there *are* differences between online advertising platforms, but those are easy enough to learn and master. And much of what works on Google's text-based advertising system, for example, could just as easily work on Bing or LinkedIn. You'll understand why as we go along.

Let's begin by taking a look at search marketing and its uses...

## *The Benefits Of Search Engine Marketing (And Similar Advertising Platforms)*

We'll start this section by acknowledging that there are a lot of business owners and marketers out there who just don't believe in paid Internet advertising, especially when it comes to search engines. Usually, this is because they've tried instituting a pay-per-click campaign before (for example, using the Google AdWords free introductory credit) and come away with the conclusion that it's too expensive, too competitive, and doesn't work. Or perhaps they've heard one too many of the stories from a friend or colleague.

Some of these criticisms are fair. Search marketing can get to be expensive very quickly, especially if you don't know what you're doing. And if you aren't paying close attention to your accounts, you can bet that some of your competitors are going to outmaneuver you.

At the same time, it's important to recognize that search marketing has some unique strengths. For one thing, it works *fast*. While it can take weeks, months, or (occasionally) even years for a search engine optimization campaign to really kick in and show a profit, search marketing campaigns can be put together and launched in a matter of minutes.

Want to earn the top spot on Google for your most important search phrases? Write a great ad, outbid your competitors, and you could have thousands of people see your marketing messages in under an hour.

That doesn't just mean you can get the bottom-line results you're looking for faster, but also that you can use new search marketing campaigns to test out keywords, concepts, and landing pages rapidly. If you don't want to go through all the trouble of launching new pages and blog posts to achieve a top search ranking without knowing whether you've chosen a good search phrase or have a winning landing page to work with, search marketing is the best way to work out any kinks in your plan before you push forward.

Search marketing campaigns are easy to tailor and adjust on the fly. If you only want certain people to see your ads, only want those ads to be displayed during certain hours, or would like to neglect certain types of prospects you don't feel are a good fit for what you have to offer, it's as easy as clicking a mouse.

Another advantage search marketing has over other tools is that you generally have more control and better analytics with paid advertising than you do with other methods. With the right tracking software, and a little time spent in your reports, you can see exactly how many people clicked on a given ad, how much time they spent on your website, where they went after they viewed your landing page, and so on. Certainly, you can get these kinds of details from other sources (something we'll look at later on), but know that you can get great statistics from your search marketing campaigns.

The bottom line is that unless you happen to be in one of those very rare markets where paid search traffic is just outrageously expensive, it's a mistake to ignore the potential of paid search positioning. Likewise, relying wholly on paid search traffic instead of investing in organic search engine optimization is likely to cost you more money over the long run than it should. Smart marketers find a balance between the two, and use both to their advantage.

## How To Set Up Efficient Search Marketing Campaigns

By this point in the book, you've probably figured out that one of the big keys to low-cost, high-ROI online marketing is being very targeted in your approach. It's all about finding your best customers and engaging them without breaking the bank. That same approach is going to carry over to search marketing.

It's important to keep that in mind, because the big mistake with search advertising – and the one that causes business owners and managers to write it off forever – is being too vague. To a certain degree, Google and the other search engines encourage this by suggesting keywords, campaigns, and bid prices to first-time users. Not knowing any better, these marketers click on lots of options, ending up with campaigns that are extraordinarily broad (and that don't appeal to any certain type of buyer at all).

You certainly can get lots of traffic to your website by putting up expensive ads and trying to convince every prospect in the world to visit your website and hear what you have to say. Most of them are still going to be a bad fit, though, and you're going to blow through your budget without seeing any firm results.

Remember in the last chapter where we looked at keyword research, and the way some popular search terms don't really indicate any real level of buying intent? That lesson is twice as important when it comes to search marketing, given that you will be paying for each visit to your website (either directly or indirectly).

With that in mind, the first step to building an efficient and profitable search marketing campaign is to choose your keywords very, very carefully. You only want to bid on terms that your *best* potential customers would search. That means skipping over those expensive keywords that generate lots and lots of traffic and focusing instead on more detailed search strings that are extremely targeted, or even closer to the long-tail end of the spectrum.

As a bonus, I should point out those lesser-searched terms tend to have much, much lower advertising costs associated with them. You'll need more of them to make your accounts profitable, of course, but it's better to put in a little bit of work researching good search marketing keywords up-front than it is to burn through your advertising budget without getting any return for your money.

Being efficient with search marketing also means taking advantage of negative keywords, which are keywords that can be used to *cancel* the display of your ad. Many advertisers never bother to take advantage of these, and that's a huge mistake. Off the top of your head, you can probably think of a few search terms right now that would indicate someone isn't a good match for what you're trying to sell. Common examples would be the word "free," as well as "cheap," or a competitor brand name. Certain locations might also be red flags.

In addition to those obvious examples, there are probably lots of search terms around your industry that indicate someone wouldn't actually be interested in buying your products or services. Suppose for a moment that you're an accountant in Miami. A keyword like "Miami accountant" could be a good fit, and "Miami small business accounting" might be even better. But "Miami accountant college" changes things pretty drastically, doesn't it? Make good use of those negative keywords so that every person who sees your ad is likely to be a possible buyer, and not someone who is researching a related topic.

Another way to ensure that your ads are being seen by the right people – and to make the most of your advertising budget – is to tweak your account settings. Google and the other search engines and social media websites give you a lot of control over the display of your ads. You can alter settings that indicate which hours you'd like them to be displayed, which geographical areas your ad should be shown to, and even what kinds of people should see your ads in the first place.

If you want them only shown in the morning to people using mobile devices, then you can set your campaigns up that way with just a few clicks. Be sure to dig into your settings and don't be afraid to experiment. That's how you're going to get the best results.

## *A Word On Social Advertising*

Although we have discussed them together so far, it's worth pointing out that social advertising (and especially ads placed on Facebook and LinkedIn) work just a little bit differently than traditional search marketing. That's because while paid search listings are typically associated with keywords, social advertising targets buyers by self-identified traits (like gender, location, industry, and so on).

That might seem like a minor difference, but it can completely alter your approach to messaging. After all, when someone enters a search string into Google or one of the other engines, you don't know much about them besides what's on their mind at the moment. With social advertising, things are reversed; you have no idea what your prospect is up to, but you can tell a great deal about their demographic background.

Where this really becomes significant is when you have a product or service that lots of people aren't aware of. When that's the case, there might be very few (or no) searches related to your product and industry. But you can still target a certain type of buyer by investing in social ad campaigns and examining the results.

As with most things, online advertising is about finding the right mix. Most small and medium-sized businesses maximize profits by experimenting with both search marketing and social ads, but using a slightly modified approach to each.

## Conversions Are Still Your Goal

If search engine optimization without conversions is useless, then search marketing without results is even worse. Never forget that every visit you get from an advertising campaign is costing you money. If that money is being spent in a way that brings you new customers, then your balance sheet is going to move in the right direction; if it doesn't, then you're essentially shoveling cash into a fire.

With that in mind, you should never set up your search marketing campaigns and forget about them. Instead, you should review the available statistics and analytics on a regular basis, and then test different elements (like headlines, offers, and so on) at regular intervals to ensure that you're turning as many visitors as possible into customers.

As you undergo this ongoing process of tweaking and testing, never forget your lesson from the earlier chapter in search engine optimization. When someone enters a phrase into a search engine, it's because they have a question or challenge that's urgent enough for them to look for an answer. The ads you put together should reflect that desire, and your landing pages should follow through in a logical way.

If someone clicks on one of your ads and is completely surprised by what they find once they arrive at your website, they are probably going to leave without figuring out what you're hoping they'll do. Put your customers first and make an effort to inform them and answer the questions *before* you start trying to persuade them to take whatever action you're hoping they'll follow through with.

A lot of marketers find that search marketing is the fastest and most efficient way to turn a targeted group of searchers into potential buyers. Even if you've never had success with paid search listings in the past, you can use them profitably now. Just know that it's going to take more than a few keywords and generic ads to achieve a high ROI.

# 5 | Target Local Buyers Online

Life is full of ironies, but few are as sharp as the fact that the World Wide Web – which has the communicative power to bring together thoughts and minds from every corner of the globe at once – has also proven itself to be an extraordinarily effective tool for reaching local buyers. The smartphone you carry around in your pocket can help you get in touch with anyone anywhere, but one of its most common tasks is replacing the Yellow Pages.

As consumers, this just comes down to a matter of convenience. We used to have to rely on billboards, printed directories, and word-of-mouth recommendations for things like restaurants and dentists. Now we can turn to the web for answers. Not only can we find more information, but also up-to-date listings with phone numbers and driving directions, and even reviews from other customers in our area.

It's hard to beat that kind of convenience.

At the same time, the fact that customers are increasingly turning to the web to find local businesses has important implications for marketers. We've already looked at the way Google and the other search engines factor geography into search results. Now it's time to see why local customers are so important, along with the best ways to reach them...

## *Local Customers Are Often The Best Customers*

Before we get into easy and cost-effective ways to target local buyers, it makes sense to say a few words about why you want them in the first place. After all, as we've already established, the Internet can be used to get buyers from anywhere in the world. Why should you care if yours are down the street or on a different continent?

In some cases, you might not. Some products and services really are so niched that geography is a secondary concern. Likewise, some types of companies are likely to serve only local customers, or at least customers who tend to be in the area at the time they are making a purchase.

If your business falls into either of those categories, then you probably already know whether local marketing is important to you or not. But for all of those in between, it's worth pointing out that local customers tend to be the best customers. They buy most often, place the biggest orders, send the most referrals, and tend to be the most profitable.

That phenomenon is easy to understand if you think about things from a psychological point of view. Most of us want to do business with other people and companies that we are familiar with. Failing that, we want to have some information that makes us feel secure that they're going to follow through on what they've promised.

That's easy to do when working with a business that's down the street, or just a few miles over. It's harder when the organization is halfway around the world, no matter how professional their website is. Local businesses just feel more familiar to us, even if we haven't worked with them before.

There are other reasons that local businesses have an advantage when it comes to earning our money, too. For one thing, it's easier to form personal relationships with business owners or sales representatives when they are located in the same area. And coordinating things like customer service and technical support is a lot easier without the added barriers of foreign languages and differing time zones (not to mention currency calculations). And of course, shipping is usually faster and less expensive within a state or region than it is across the country or farther.

Probably the biggest strength, however, is that local companies tend to know what we want because they are seeing and hearing the same things we are every day. That's an advantage you just can't duplicate no matter how much you spend on market research.

As a business owner or executive, each of these facts represents good news for you. That's because local buyers don't just make the best customers, they also happen to be the easiest and most inexpensive to reach.

When you target local customers, you have a lot of advantages working in your favor. Google and the other search engines will prioritize your webpages for local searchers. You can use your social networking accounts to connect with your best customers and know that, if they are in the same geographic region, they probably have contacts in the area, as well. And by restricting your advertising accounts to a certain city or area, you can limit costs while gaining more visibility than your competitors.

With all of these issues working in your favor, it makes no sense to ignore your local market. Let's move on and see how you can get buyers in your neighborhood to notice your company on the Internet.

## How To Target Local Customers Online

Of all the low-cost, high-ROI Internet marketing strategies you can put to use, targeting local buyers is perhaps the simplest. In fact, just adding things like a mailing address, city name, and driving directions to your website could be enough for Google to recognize your location and start sending searchers your way.

Even though that gives you a positive start, however, there is a lot more you can do to help your own cause. Some of the best practices around local online marketing simply build on those search visibility steps, and can have a very big impact.

For instance, once you've added geographic keywords to your website to make sure that buyers in your neighborhood can find you online, why not take the next logical step and make it simple for them to find you in real life, too? Telephone numbers and driving directions are a good start, but you should also include maps, photos, and possibly even nearby landmarks on your website if you're expecting drive-in customers or retail foot traffic.

Another good step you can take is to make sure your business has listings with all industry and neighborhood review websites. Yelp is a big one, of course, as is TripAdvisor, if you're in an area frequented by tourists. We'll talk about reviews and the enormous impact they can have on your business later, but for now you should be sure that your company is well-represented on these sites, with good photos, current contact information, and lots of details that show what sets your company apart.

Once you have profiles on local review sites like Yelp, invite your best customers to use them. Even just a few positive testimonials can go a long way toward convincing potential buyers who are on the fence to give you a shot.

If you have specialized industry websites in your area, be sure to take advantage of those, as well. Because a lot of your competitors are going to neglect them, registering gives you a chance to get ahead. On the one hand, you might be the only business in your neighborhood with a completed profile. And for another, good directories amount to verifiable information, which can factor into search engine rankings.

If local customers have access to products, prices, or discounts that other buyers don't, consider creating special pages just for them. As with most of the tactics in this book, this has both an immediate and a long-term benefit. On the surface, it gives local customers another reason to either visit your retail location or come back to your website again in the future. And in the bigger picture, it gives you another destination for search engine spiders and social media links.

Another Internet marketing best practice is to separate your promotional and advertising campaigns by geographic area. If you have followed along this far, it won't surprise you to know that you should take care to appeal to your most important buyers (geography included) by targeting your ads and messages directly to them. That means setting up separate ad groups, offers, and landing pages for buyers based on where they live or do business.

And finally, if you have several different locations, or serve several different areas, consider setting up different webpages (or even entire websites) for each area. This might seem like a lot of extra work when you're getting started, but doing so will allow you to target each distinct customer base more carefully, to save money in your overall marketing budget, and to more easily segment your analytics over different geographic zones.

In other words, it's going to give you a way to reach out to local buyers in different areas and track the results. Building and maintaining separate websites obviously isn't going to be a feasible answer for every small or medium-sized business, but it's worth discussing with your web design team if your customers are spread out over many different locales.

## Use Offline Strategies For Online Promotion

As I noted earlier in the book, Internet marketing has largely displaced a lot of the old standby promotional techniques smaller businesses used to count on. But it didn't kill them altogether, and you can use offline tactics to support your online strategy.

One good example of this is the way you often see businesses hand out printed flyers that have basic information about the company, coupons, and even contact details. All of this is standard offline sales activity. But by including things like a web address, a reminder about the company's mobile webpage, references to online reviews, or even a QR code that takes users to an online store, marketers are bringing offline prospects into their digital sales funnels.

Promoting your online content in print works in other ways, too. You can include web addresses and social identifiers in local print ads, or make reference to your online presence in a direct mail piece.

Another great two-way marketing tactic is to use the local press to get the word out about your company. By simply calling an editor, or issuing a press release, you may be able to get a story written about your business. That kind of attention is usually good for your sales and credibility, but it could also lead to follow-up stories and blog posts being placed on the publications website. Those, in turn, generate high-quality links back to your website and help your search engine positioning.

The point to take away from all of this is that your website is built to do a lot of jobs. It can be a salesperson, a PR agent, recruiter, and a customer service specialist all in one. By promoting it offline, you increase the odds that you can bring new visitors to your most powerful business tool. And, provided that you know who your best prospects are and have followed the advice given up to this point, good things are going to happen when they find your web presence.

# 6 | Use Social Media To
# Build Buzz

At the time of this writing, social media marketing is the "it" strategy that all business owners and managers seem to want to master… even if they aren't quite sure what that means.

Part of the confusion has to do with the fact that social networking websites like Facebook, Twitter, and LinkedIn have exploded in the past few years. With billions of users between them, they've become a part of everyday life in a way that few people expected five or ten years ago.

Another part of the confusion, however, comes from a bit of ambiguity about social media marketing goals. Nearly every business person agrees that social media should be taken advantage of, given that customers and colleagues are using these sites every day. What few can agree on, though, is the best way to do that, and what a successful outcome even looks like.

There are a lot of companies "doing" social media marketing even though they can't point to any tangible benefits. Certainly, some businesses will point to the fact that they have thousands of followers, or that they send a lot of tweets, but are those *really* positive indicators? They suggest that people might be paying at least a little bit of attention, but how often does that attention turn into real, measurable bottom-line improvement?

Because this is a book on getting the most out of Internet marketing with the least amount of waste, I don't want you doing anything that isn't going to profit your company and bring you closer to your goals. So let's take a look at how you can build a commonsense social strategy that helps generate the kinds of results you can believe in...

## What Is Social Media Marketing Good For?

One of the biggest reasons business people struggle with social media marketing is that they want to treat it like search engine optimization or search marketing. That is, they want to use profiles on sites like Facebook and Twitter to drive traffic to targeted landing pages, and then use conventional conversion strategies.

That *can* work, but it's not usually your best approach. To find the reason why, we only have to go back a few chapters to our insights on searcher intent.

When someone enters a search string into Google, it's because they have a particular problem or idea in mind. Even if they aren't thinking about buying a product or service, they are looking for a solution of some sort. That's not necessarily true in a social networking site, where people tend to spend time catching up with friends and family, trading jokes, learning more about their interests, and otherwise having fun.

In this context, they aren't as open to marketing messages because those aren't being perceived as information or solutions, just interruptions that are getting in the way of their more leisurely activities.

Savvy social marketers understand that, and go out of their way to grab interest and attention without overwhelming fans and followers with sales-related content. There are exceptions to this rule, of course, and instances where you'll want to issue social posts that essentially amount to a call to action (more on this later). Do it too fast or too often, though, and you'll likely find your fans and followers are tuning you out.

So instead of focusing on transactions, look for opportunities to grab interest and build relationships. Engage customers one-on-one, especially when they ask you questions or try to involve you in a discussion. Resist the urge to jump into sales mode and start telling them about all the great things you have to sell.

If you're feeling like relationship-building is a rather soft goal, and one that's hard to measure, you're certainly right. We'll get to the things you can do to monetize your social following in a bit, and then look at some ways you can check up on the results. For now, just understand that attention and interest are the currencies you spend and earn on social media sites. Gaining them both should be your first priority.

To sum this idea up, social media is good for a lot of things, but direct selling usually isn't one of them. You can use your social accounts to make new acquaintances, familiarize prospects with your industry, give a behind-the-scenes look at your business, and even address customer request and recruiting concerns. But, if you treat your social accounts as nothing more than a megaphone to broadcast your latest deals and specials, you're probably going to come up a bit short of the results you're hoping for.

## The First Steps To A Successful Social Campaign

As an individual, you can pick up your phone, take a quick snapshot of yourself, and have a more or less personalized social media profile online and active in just a few minutes. As a marketer, you are free to take the same approach, but that would be a very bad idea.

That's because the very first step to a successful social media marketing campaign is ensuring that your business (along with your key personnel) can be found on all the major social sites. At a minimum, you want to be present on Facebook, Twitter, LinkedIn, and Google+.

Being present isn't the same as being accounted for, however, and a blank business listing that lacks a logo and personalized page sends a bad message. It's almost worse than having no profile at all. When potential customers come across your social accounts and see nothing, one of two things happens: Either they think they've got the wrong company, or they wonder whether you're still in operation.

Obviously, neither of these outcomes is going to move you closer to your business goals. So it's worth taking the time to complete and update your accounts. At a minimum, you want the visitor to be able to tell who you are, where you're located, what you do, and how they can contact your business. It's even better if you can add a few succinct descriptions and high-quality photos.

As we mentioned earlier in the chapter on setting up your website, it's not a bad idea to have a professional photographer come by your place of business and snap a few shots. They'll look great on your homepage, and even better on your social profiles.

If the thought of putting time, effort, and money into your business social networking pages seems like something you don't want to do, consider what happens when someone is referred to your business. They are very likely to type your name into a Google search box, or to look you up on their favorite social media platform. Either way, what they find could determine whether they decide to take the next step or not.

To finish that idea, it's worth pointing out that your social profiles can actually outrank your company's website in the search engine listings, especially if your website is new or has been recently overhauled. It's not at all unusual, for example, for professionals to be easier to find on LinkedIn than they are on their own websites. If you're tempted to use a quick snapshot and a few bullet points instead of getting a quality headshot and proofreading your bio, know that someday soon that decision might cost you sales and networking opportunities that you'll never know about.

## How To Grow Your Network And Influence Buyers

Once you have your completed social networking accounts in place, it's time to start growing your list of contacts. Luckily, this is a lot easier than a lot of people might think.

The first step is to go with what you know. That is, leverage your existing relationships and partnerships on social media sites. Even the most overwhelmed and reclusive among us tend to have a few friends, relatives, and colleagues we can get in touch with. Make sure they are all added through your company's social networking pages. Better yet, see if you can get them to write you endorsements and testimonials.

From there, the next step is to go to your second generation of contacts. That is, individuals that your peers and acquaintances are already connected to who might be familiar with your business. Go ahead and add them too, because most of them will feel comfortable adding you back if they see you are somehow affiliated with a person they already trust. That's how social media works.

After that, you can continue branching out to new layers of contacts, but a faster way to gain friends and followers is to start sharing content that's relevant to your business or industry. The last part of that sentence is very important, because you don't want just anyone in your social network, regardless of how it might seem in the beginning when you only have a few followers. Remember our rule about your best potential customers: If someone doesn't fit that profile, they're probably going to be more of a hassle than they are worth in the long run.

By sharing ideas and participating in discussions, you'll start to catch the attention of those who are actively interested in what you have to offer, and can establish a bit of credibility for your business, too. Remember, though, that we are looking for interest and attention. Dry business articles will interest a few people, but ideas that have a bit of humor, edge, or timeliness to them are more likely to get followers clicking. And don't forget that you can mix up formats – sometimes photos and videos will get a much bigger response in social media than simple text will.

As long as you can be persistent with your posting and stay on message, you'll eventually reach a point where you have a lot of people interested in what you have to say (and many of them will be good prospects for your company). This can take weeks or even months, and it's frustrating when you're just getting started. Remember, though, that social networking is a lot like real-life networking, in that it can take a while to make a memorable impression on lots of people.

One last point before we move on to the next topic: Don't forget that social media is a two-way street of communication. Posting and getting involved is important, but so is listening and paying attention to what's going on around you. A lot of the best connections and business opportunities you'll form online will come about because of something you see or read, not what you post. Pay attention to what other people are working on, too, because it might lead to an inspiration, or even a brand-new customer.

## Don't Be Too Social With Social

A funny thing sometimes happens to people, even professionals, when they go on social media. Namely, that they seem to lose their minds and/or forget that what they've posted could be shared with the public (if it isn't already).

This is reflected in celebrity scandals all the time. Hardly a week goes by when a Hollywood star doesn't accidentally send out "private" photos, a married politician is caught hitting on a follower, or a well-known media personality is questioned about some radical political or religious opinions that have been shared.

The same thing happens, dozens of times a day, with business owners and managers. The situation is different, though, because it isn't reported in the news... it's just shared with family, friends, and customers. The other difference is that while most of us forget about the actor, politician, or newscaster who slips up when the next scandal comes along, we *always* remember something about a person we know and work with.

Consider this my not-so-subtle advice to avoid being *too* social on social media. Obviously, you have a right to be an individual, express your opinions, and enjoy yourself, but take the appropriate precautions. For starters, it's a good idea to keep your personal and professional profiles separate, and to update your privacy settings so that not everyone you work with can dig into the details of your home life. Beyond that, remember that anything posted to the Internet can eventually become public, and that many potential customers and partners will judge you based on what they read online.

If you have a habit of posting or commenting on material that's inflammatory, politically charged, racy, or otherwise controversial, it could end up costing you a lot of money.

You might think that no one cares what you post on social media, or that all of your friends and customers agree with you anyway. And you might be right. But once again, I want you to remember that a lot of the biggest losses associated with poor Internet marketing and social media are never seen or realized. They show up in the order you don't get, the vendor who won't work with you, or the customer who decides to take their business to someone who hasn't offended them without ever saying why.

## Monetize Social Followers By Generating A Bit Of Buzz

With that caveat about personal and professional social media behavior out of the way, it's time to get down to the business of actually turning your social following into a real business asset. The best way to do that is by generating some kind of buzz.

In this context, buzz is simply anything that gets people buzzing. It could be an in-store event, an unforgettable deal, or a campaign that makes people stop and laugh. If our attention for social media marketing success is based on interest, then the next step is turning that interest into action.

Sometimes, that can be as simple as noting on your social accounts that you have a new product, or a very big sale. If your network is filled with the kind of people who are very interested in what you have to offer, they may be curious enough to click through to your website and eventually contact or place an order.

But if your contacts are a little less focused and/or committed, it might take something special. You could host a contest, create a viral video clip, or make a big announcement. The specific method isn't what's important – the idea that you have something that your followers will pay attention to and pass along to *their* followers is.

The best thing about social media, besides the one-on-one communication style it affords, is that the ideas that are fun and insightful can be shared so quickly and with so many people. In that sense, you aren't trying to inform your followers as much as you are trying to start a fire. You want the interest to keep burning from one reader to the next.

For that to have any impact on your business, there has to be one final step: a strong call to action. After you've engaged your prospects and gotten them interested in what you have to say, see if you can get them to take the next step. That might be signing up for your email newsletter, making a small purchase, or printing out a coupon that they can bring to your store (as examples).

Whatever this step is, it's going to be the action item that helps you turn interested people into possible buyers. Accordingly, it's also the step that you have to scrutinize closely with analytics. If you find that contacts (and even their contacts) are responding well to your offers, you know you are making some headway with your social media campaigns; if not, it might be time to devote your time and energy elsewhere.

A lot of business people love social media marketing because it's inexpensive and gives them a reason to log in to Facebook from the office.

But if you aren't getting results, then you aren't really marketing, are you?

The only way to turn your social following into a business asset is to be persistent, stay on message, and especially to study the results and tweak your approach going forward.

# 7 | Your Email List Is Digital Gold

Like search engine optimization, email newsletters have been a cornerstone of Internet marketing for a long time. And, just like SEO, email has been changing in ways that are making it hard for some businesses to keep up.

The problem isn't that email is going away; if anything, it's that people are using it *too much*. Most of us send and receive so many messages on a daily and weekly basis that it's hard to keep up with items that are directed to us personally, much less an avalanche of announcements and newsletters.

As a result, buyers are subscribing to fewer email newsletters, and devoting less time and attention to the ones they are still signed up for. At a time when email delivery is getting to be more reliable and less expensive, contacts are disappearing and click-through rates are declining.

It's not all bad news, though. While customers are giving up some email newsletters, that leaves bigger opportunities for marketers who are keeping their subscribers interested. And, if you can do that, the rewards are incredible.

In this chapter, we're going to take a quick look at why email marketing still works, and works extremely well. Then, we are going to examine some strategies you can use to attract subscribers and then turn them into buyers using one of the most cost-effective Internet marketing tools ever devised...

## *Why Email Marketing Works*

Although it might not seem as sexy as some other Internet marketing tools, email is consistent, accessible, and low-cost. You can send entire campaigns for what you'd spend on a few search marketing clicks in some markets, all while reaching hundreds or thousands of subscribers at once.

You get a longer message with a well-crafted email than you would a tweet or social post, and lots of people who don't bother with Facebook and wouldn't click through to your blog will check out an item that lands in their inbox, especially if it has a subject line that interests them.

All of this put together means that email is the perfect medium for keeping in touch with customers, making sure they know about what's going on with you and your business, and generating a quick splash of sales while spending next to nothing in terms of time and money.

For any of that to happen, though, you need a list of subscribers. And any list won't do – you want one filled with your very best customers.

## Email List-Building Made Easy

Admittedly, finding targeted subscribers for your email list is the hardest part of the process, especially given the challenges I've already addressed. Most people feel like they are getting too many emails already, so getting them to sign up for even more isn't all that straightforward.

But that doesn't mean you can't build up an email list quickly. All you have to do is think like your prospect and answer the question, "What's in it for me?" Looking at things from that perspective, you can discover that there are lots of different ways to get people to sign up.

One tried and proven way to get subscribers is by hosting events, online and off, and asking interested people to join your list to get future updates. Things like seminars and demonstrations can be a great way to attract interest and bring in new subscribers.

You can also try trading something of value for a valid email address. For example, lots of businesses set up landing pages where they offer free reports, videos, and recordings that are only available to subscribers. Provided these downloads have enough value, they can be used to get hundreds or thousands of people to sign up in a short period of time.

Letting buyers know that you offer discounts through your email newsletter is yet another way to generate interest. If people like what you have to sell, and think they can save money by reading your newsletters, they probably will.

You can sometimes build a great email list by borrowing someone else's. By that, I mean that you can take advantage of affiliate marketing opportunities (possibly by combining this technique with the ones listed above) and get someone else's subscribers to join your list.

And finally, there are lots of old-school marketing tactics that still work when it comes to getting email addresses. You've probably seen bowls full of business cards, and gotten business-to-business telemarketing calls asking you to provide an email address for follow-up quotes and literature. These can be great for increasing the size of your subscriber list quickly.

Once you start brainstorming ideas, it turns out there are an almost endless number of ways to add new subscribers. The one thing you should never, do, though, is pay for lists scraped off of websites or add subscribers without their permission. Doing so isn't just annoying – it can be a violation of various laws in several different countries (and could cost you millions in fines).

I should also point out that you may need to keep more than one email list. Earlier, I asked you to identify your most important groups of customers and prospects. If the profiles you came up with have different needs and interests, then it might make sense to maintain separate email newsletters for each of them. Segmenting your lists is a great way to tailor your messaging to a specific audience and achieve higher click-through rates.

Of course, getting email newsletter subscribers is one thing, and keeping them is another. And motivating them to take action when you send a message is yet a third challenge.

In fact, I often like to think of email marketing in terms of those three goals: *keeping subscribers you have, getting them to pay attention while reminding them that you're there, and then persuading them to take the next step.*

Let's examine each of these goals briefly.

## *Making Sure You Don't Lose Subscribers*

First, we want to keep the subscribers we have. That sounds simple, but a lot of marketers unintentionally annoy their subscribers, causing them to opt out of the list. There are a lot of things that bother people, but when it comes to email there are usually a few culprits: sending emails too often, making your emails too sales-oriented, and sending low-quality emails.

In terms of frequency, most businesses can get away with emailing subscribers once every week or two. Some can pull off twice-a-week emails, but only if the messages are stocked with great content (more on that in a second). Except during unusual times, like the days leading up to an event, you shouldn't try to get in touch with your subscribers more often than that.

When emails are too pushy, they read like straight up advertisements. Ask yourself: Would you sign up to read more advertisements every day? Guess what, your subscribers won't either. If they feel like you are only sending the messages because you want their money, they'll take their time and attention elsewhere.

Quality can be measured in a few different ways. Obviously, using good visuals and layouts for your email marketing messages is critical, but so are things like grammar and proofreading. Subscribers will forgive a lot, but not incoherent messages that don't make sense. And while you're at it, ensure that every marketing email you send is mobile-friendly. Remember that smartphone and tablet users make up more than half of your customers, and use templates that display well on those devices.

## Engaging Subscribers So They Read Your Messages

I've already mentioned that your email shouldn't be straight-up advertisements (or at least that most of them shouldn't be). So, what kind of content can you include that *will* make subscribers take notice?

The best way to engage customers and potential customers through emails is by sharing articles that appeal to them. You want to give them lots of fresh, timely, and interesting content. Think about the way magazines (which make their money off of advertisements) pull in readers: They include juicy articles, aimed at a specific type of person.

You can do the same. In fact, you'll probably have an easier time than most magazine editors do, because you are only trying to come up with content – be it articles, pictures, or other materials – that appeal to your very best customers. They don't have to work for anyone else.

Even if you don't read many magazines yourself, coming up with attention-grabbing titles is an industry standard practice. You should work to make the titles of your newsletter articles irresistible, and then put them in your email subject lines. That way, when they arrive in the subscriber's inbox, the recipient will be so curious that they won't be able to stop themselves from having a look.

Also, don't think you have to spend all of your time generating lengthy pieces of content for your email newsletter. Generally speaking, shorter articles work best. As a rule of thumb, if you need to go longer than a few hundred words, it's best to shorten your article for your email and then add a link to a longer version of the same content that's on your website. If your emails are too long, many subscribers won't even bother reading them because they'll immediately jump to the conclusion that they don't have the time.

So if you can generate some top 10 lists, infographics, introductory guides, and product reviews, you're well on the way to building a successful and profitable email marketing campaign. These types of content won't sell anything by themselves, of course, but they will get your subscribers reading and thinking. From there, it's only natural that they take the next step.

## Getting Subscribers To Take Action

The goal of every email newsletter you send is to create some kind of action. It's worth noting, however, that the action doesn't necessarily have to be a completed sale. Depending on the way your online marketing plans are structured, you might ask readers to click through to a landing page, follow you on a social network, RSVP for an upcoming event, or do something else. Often, setting an appointment or making a purchase will be your ultimate call to action, but don't necessarily assume that has to be the case.

As for the call to action itself, that should be simple, and it should follow naturally with the content of the message itself. For example, a beauty shop might send an email newsletter with the subject line and leading article of "5 Fruits That Make You Feel and Look Younger." The call to action at the end of the piece could be a coupon for a rejuvenating skin treatment, or an upcoming seminar on clean eating.

Imagine, though, if the same type of article ended with an invitation to come and enjoy a discounted oil change. Such a transition wouldn't make any sense, and email subscribers might not even trust health advice coming from their local auto service station.

That's a somewhat silly example, but it's not as far-fetched as you might think. Lots of businesses send out emails that seem to have nothing to do with what they are offering. The farther you get from your products and services in your email articles, the lower click-through rates and conversions are going to be.

You already know your best customers. When looking to take advantage of email marketing, give them the content they want and then make an offer that fits in with your Internet marketing goals *and* their wants or needs.

If you can manage to build a list of good prospects and customers, engage them with insightful content on a regular basis, and use smart calls to action at the end of each message, you'll discover what hundreds of other business owners and managers already know – email still is one of the fastest and most efficient ways to sell products and services in the digital age.

# 8 | Build And Grow A Great
# Online Reputation

In the last few years, online reputation management has gone from a relatively unknown specialty to a mainstream business topic. And it tends to impact small and medium-sized businesses more than anyone else.

That's because online reputation management is really just an old idea brought into the Internet age. Back before we had Google and social networks, we had something simpler: "word-of-mouth advertising." Your online reputation is simply the sum total of that word-of-mouth, but put on the Internet for the world to see.

Think about this way: There's a good chance that every review, testimonial, referral, complaint, and shred of feedback that has been with your business over the past decade has found its way online. And once it did, it became something that potential customers, vendors, partners, and job seekers can see when they investigate your company.

Is it any surprise that your sales can rise and fall based on what people see when they look you up on Google, LinkedIn, or elsewhere?

Whereas someone interested in a restaurant down the street might have once asked friends to see if anyone they knew had eaten there, now it takes mere seconds to type the business name into Google and see details about the menu, prices, and other diners' opinions. In fact, some people won't try a new product or vendor until they've done a thorough bit of research online.

The things that are posted about you and your business (and sometimes *by* you and your business) on the Internet are a big deal. In this chapter, we're going to look at what you can do to shape your online reputation in a positive way and then use all of that positive feedback to drive new opportunities...

## Discover Your Online Reputation By Searching Like A Customer

How often do you perform a Google search on your own name, your company's name, and your own products or services? If you're like most of the business owners I meet with, it's something you've done once or twice out of curiosity and then not thought about again.

That's understandable, but it can leave you in a situation where you don't actually discover a problem with your own online reputation until someone either tells you about it or sales drop off suddenly and you get curious enough to have a look.

To have a good idea of what customers are seeing when they look up your business online – and remember, they *will* look before they decide to do business with you – you have to search like they would.

The first step in that activity is to do just what I described, and search your business name on Google as well as the other major engines. Go beyond the first couple of pages of results, and keep looking until you start running into things that aren't relevant to your company at all. Next, look up your business on Facebook, Twitter, LinkedIn, and Google+.

As you follow this exercise, make note of anything you see that might affect someone's first impressions of your company, be it positive or negative. At the same time, don't assume that no news is good news. If your business is hard to find online, that's not exactly a ringing endorsement for what you sell or offer.

Once you have a good idea of what's posted about your business, repeat the same steps using your own name, and the names of any of your key personnel. The smaller your business is, the more likely it is that people will associate leadership with the company and its products or services. In that way, there can be a bleed-over effect, where negative information about a person ends up hurting an entire organization.

## *Getting Started: Set Up Profiles And Remove Any Red Flags*

Once you are aware of what your online reputation is like, it's time to start getting proactive about improving things. A good way to begin that process is by making sure that both you and your company are easy to find.

If you didn't take my advice earlier in the book to set up profiles for your company on leading industry and social media websites, stop reading and go do it now. Every one of these directories is an opportunity to meet new buyers, and to shape the messaging that's out there about your business. Plus, social profiles and industry directory listings can out-rank your website, or at least show up on the first page of search rankings. Make sure they have up-to-date details that put your company in the best possible light.

Once you have taken that step, it's time to return to those problem areas you identified. Maybe these were bad reviews left by former customers, so-so feedback contributed by people who don't really understand what you do (or have mistaken you for another company), or even angry posts trashing your business that were written by former employees.

Assuming that these are online for everyone to find and see, you need to minimize the damage they can cause. Contrary to popular belief, that does not mean you should become angry and emotional, or attack the person who wrote the review.

You see business owners make this mistake all the time, and it only serves to make it seem like the original reviewer was correct, and that the business owner is likely to overreact to criticism. So whatever you do, stay calm and resist the urge to come out swinging.

A much better option is to follow a calm and reasoned plan for clearing up confusion and disagreements. The first step is to find out whether the negative reviewer's feedback is accurate. If it is, or if the person who posted it thought it was, then consider contacting them directly to apologize. That can be a difficult step to take, mentally and emotionally, but it serves a couple of purposes.

On the one hand, when you apologize for not meeting someone's expectations, it tends to take away their anger. And when that happens, they will usually refrain from writing further negative reviews about your company. On the other hand, a direct dialogue with someone who isn't happy with you might be painful, but it can give you a chance to make things right. Do that successfully, and they might even retract their review altogether... or write a new, better version.

Assuming that isn't possible, your next step is to politely tell your side of the story. Most reviews on industry websites (like Yelp, for example) will allow businesses to add feedback to reviews. So, if there was some kind of misunderstanding, cheerfully explain what you think happened and the steps your business is taking to resolve the issue going forward.

Again, this might feel like an unnecessary step if you don't think you've done anything wrong, but know that the public is more inclined to believe another customer than they are a business owner or manager. Issuing an online apology shows that you take customer satisfaction carefully, and that you're paying attention to what people say online. Besides, having a bad online review with a follow-up is better than letting it stand on its own in perpetuity.

Finally, if neither of those two steps works, or if the review is just so outlandish and incorrect that there's little question about its accuracy, then you can contact the website that hosts the review in the first place and ask them to retract what has been posted. They are likely to decline unless there's a good reason (for instance, if you can prove that the review was written by a competitor or someone who hasn't ever done business with you), but it's the last-resort step worth pursuing when you don't have any other options.

## Get Your Best Customers
## To Say Good Things

Once you've made an attempt to clear up any trouble areas with your online reputation, it's time to go on a charm offensive. When a potential customer or employee looks up your business online, you want them to find out about all of the great things you've done. In order for that to happen, you're going to have to get in touch with the people closest to your business and ask them to sing your praises.

Luckily, most good customers (not to mention vendors and former employees) are going to be open to taking one or two minutes to post a review of your business if you treated them well and fairly. Many would probably have done so already if they knew how important it is to the future of your company.

The key to pulling this off is not to make too much of a big deal about it. Instead of begging and pleading for five-star testimonials, simply ask people who are known to be fans of your business if they wouldn't mind sharing a few words about their experiences on Yelp, TripAdvisor, or whatever website is most meaningful to you and your customers.

It only takes a few good reviews to make a big impression on prospects. And the more reviews you get, the more likely it is that other people will decide to share their thoughts, as well. Feedback tends to be contagious that way. Why not get the ball rolling by asking your best customers to say a few good things?

## Ask And Advertise

Because momentum builds when it comes to favorability and impressions, you should encourage buyers to add their own feedback on a regular basis. This isn't difficult to do, and can even be automated.

As an example, you could thank customers for their business and request that they leave reviews for you at a specific website on a printed receipt. Or, you could attach a notice at the bottom of each email newsletter pointing out that you love to get endorsements on LinkedIn.

You won't want to go overboard, of course (remember, annoying customers is never a good idea), but don't be shy about letting buyers know how much their reviews and support mean to you. They probably don't realize just how much of an impact their testimonials can have on your sales, so feel free to educate them in this area.

Things work the other way, too. Once you have built up enough of a positive online reputation, you can start to show it off and use it as a sales tool. For example, if 98% of online reviewers say they would work with you again, why not include that fact on your website, or in your email signature? People trust the opinions of other people, so if you have some great stats or honors to show off, use them to keep impressions moving in the right direction.

Just as a final thought to this section, beware of anyone who offers to help you add lots of online reviews for your business in a short amount of time. Posting false reviews is a dangerous strategy. The FTC has recently made a point of designating these kinds of activities outright fraud, and getting caught with fake feedback could get you permanently blacklisted from a lot of leading websites, too.

## Build A Business That Deserves Praise And You'll Get it

Once you've started asking customers for their public support, there is another trick you can use to establish and grow a positive online reputation that doesn't require you to request a single review ever again: Just build the kind of business that stands out in people's minds.

In other words, if you want five-star reviews, get in the habit of providing five-star service.

It might sound silly to say so, but building a positive online reputation really is that simple. Customers will typically go public with their thoughts for one of two reasons: because they were very impressed, or very disappointed. And of course, the disappointing reviews tend to be noticed and remembered more than the positive ones.

Consistently earn high marks for things like customer service and fair pricing, however, and people start to notice. They'll trust you more, respond to your marketing faster, and be predisposed to saying good things about your company themselves. All you have to do to make that happen is earn that great reputation in the first place.

Never forget that your online reputation is really just word-of-mouth advertising spread to the digital age. Pay attention to what customers are saying about you, online and off, and check back at regular intervals to see if anything is changed. Don't be afraid to admit mistakes and give your side of the story when it's needed. And above all else, provide the kind of service that makes buyers want to tell the whole world about how great you are.

# 9 | Wash, Rinse, Repeat: Regularly Review Strategy And Analytics

No matter how carefully you follow the tips outlined so far in this book, there's a good chance something in your Internet marketing plan won't go the way you expect. Perhaps you'll find that you just aren't climbing the search engine rankings the way you expected, or the new visitors to your website aren't responding and converting at a rate that makes your plans profitable. Or, maybe things go well until something changes (like advertising costs or email delivery success rates).

When these kinds of issues come up, it isn't just that a change in course is required – you have to know what you're fixing, why, and where to turn next.

Unfortunately, a lot of business owners and executives find themselves feeling "stuck" when their Internet marketing campaigns go off course. With their best-laid plans crumbling to ashes, they can't figure out whether they should move right or left, and so they keep plowing straight… compounding losses and losing customers because they aren't sure where they went wrong.

The only way to avoid making these kinds of mistakes is to have a sense of what's working and what isn't. And that means reviewing both strategy and analytics, which we will examine in this chapter...

## Why Analytics Are So Important

Most Internet marketing campaigns, even successful ones, are built on what could accurately be called "best guesses." That is, business owners and managers brainstorm ideas about who they *think* their best customers are, what they *think* those people want, and the messages they *imagine* will grab their attention.

Often enough, these impressions turn out to be dead on. Once in a while, though, things look very different in retrospect. Looking back, it might be obvious why something didn't work, but it's never so apparent when you're making the decision in the first place (otherwise, there wouldn't be much of a decision to make).

The point I'm driving at is that not all of your ideas will turn out to be winners. That's okay. Having a few miscues won't ruin your company forever... but sticking with them after they've proven to be unsuccessful *will*.

That's precisely why web analytics are so important. By installing a few simple lines of code on each webpage (either through Google's free analytics tool or another package), you can get a close-up view of what actions visitors are taking when they come to your website.

Most of the people who visit your pages and don't buy, or even return, won't ever tell you why. They might not even know themselves. For that matter, most of your web visitors who become good customers won't tell you why, either.

With a good web analytics package in place, that doesn't matter. You can study aggregate data from all the visitors to your website and draw your own conclusions. That is, so long as you have an analytics package installed, use it regularly, and know what you're looking for.

## What Can You Learn From Web Analytics?

Almost every business website has some kind of analytics software installed. But at the same time, having one and using it isn't the same thing.

At most, the majority of business owners tend to look at their analytics once every few months or so to see whether web visits are up or down, and to figure out what kinds of keywords customers are using to find their websites. That's important information, but it's really only the tip of the iceberg when it comes to what your analytics software has to tell you.

By going a little bit deeper, you can find out who is coming to your website, where they're coming from (both geographically and on the web), which pages they are spending time on, how much time they're spending on those pages, how they are navigating through your website, and so much more.

In other words, your web analytics can tell you what your customers want, and which parts of your website they like and don't like. That's exactly the kind of information you need to attract more of your best customers and become more profitable, and yet that data often goes ignored by the people who need it the most.

Trying to find new customers online without paying attention to web analytics is like going on a cross-country road trip and taking a compass instead of your smartphone. All the things you want to know about building a smarter, leaner business are right there in front of you, but you have to take time to look for what you need.

That, of course, is why so many business people get tripped up when it comes to web analytics. Because the data is presented in charts, figures, and statistics – not to mention web jargon – it can seem confusing (at best) or intimidating (at worst). Most business owners and managers don't have time for all the things they already understand, so they certainly can't find lots of hours in the day to look at a bunch of numbers and figures that seem overwhelming.

As understandable as that mindset is, it's akin to saying that you don't want to review your profit and loss statements because accounting is hard. There is a learning curve when it comes to learning web analytics, but it's not nearly as steep as you might think, and the rewards are immense.

Spend just a couple of hours understanding key terms and indicators, and you'll quickly develop a sense for the health of your website and Internet marketing campaigns. You only need a few general concepts to navigate your way around the numbers, and these are the keys to find out what buyers really want from you and your company.

## Eliminating Bottlenecks And Finding Opportunities

How does analytic data from your website go from being "interesting" to becoming "actionable"? By helping you to identify bottlenecks and opportunities.

Bottlenecks or dead ends are places on your website where visitors simply stop or leave. For example, if you have a great search marketing campaign in place, but visitors aren't moving past your landing pages (or certain points on your landing pages), then you have a bottleneck and it's costing you lots of money.

Without examining the analytic data, you would know that you aren't seeing a return on your advertising investment, but you wouldn't know why. By digging into the relevant statistics, on the other hand, you can see that potential customers are leaving after they see the price of your product (as an example), or when they see it isn't available for immediate shipping.

Armed with this kind of information, you could make tweaks to your landing pages, such as adding to a list of features to increase value, offering a discount for first-time buyers, or giving more detailed inventory and delivery information.

Even the best websites can have bottlenecks in several places. With a close look at your web analytics, you could find that buyers aren't converting because they need answers to frequently asked questions (in the form of a new page), or aren't being impressed by what they find on your website "about" section. Again, these are only simple examples, but they illustrate a larger point: Without the right data, you would only be guessing at the root cause behind these types of issues.

It's worth pointing out that web analytics can help you spot opportunities as well as problems. When visitors come to your website after looking for certain search terms, spend lots of time on a particular subject, or return to one section again and again, that's a sign that you need more content or resources that appeal to those ideas or motivations. In the same way that we can't know at the outset which of our ideas or preconceived notions won't work out, neither can we always anticipate just how powerful some promotions will turn out to be.

If there is a sudden uptick in traffic or conversions, you want to know where it's coming from. If you weren't sure, you might be tempted to double down on a tactic or investment that wasn't working, or miss a chance to try something with the potential to bring you great success.

Eliminating bottlenecks and finding opportunities are really two sides of the same coin, and they all point toward one distinct goal: making your website more effective and efficient. Wouldn't it be worth spending a little time on analytics charts and numbers if it meant being able to find more of your best customers and figure out how you can serve them better?

## Failing To Plan Is Planning To Fail

Another reason to get up close and personal with your analytics data is to periodically review your Internet marketing campaigns.

While this book is heavy on strategy and light on technical details, it would be a mistake to think that those details don't matter at all. Things like social media policies and search algorithms change all the time, and your approach to finding customers online needs to change with them. As a result, you'll need to review what you're doing – and the results – at least a couple of times a year.

You can also take it as a given that your business won't remain static, either. You'll think of new ideas, launch new products and services, go after new customers, and change personnel. That's just part of the business of being in business. With each of these changes, though, you'll have a slightly different outlook on the future of your company, as well as a handful of new priorities.

Most businesses, even those with long histories, are in a state of constant flux. If ongoing shifts and evolutions aren't being reflected on a company's website, then pages and content quickly go out of date. Even worse, messaging and campaigns stop being as effective as they could be. If you don't refresh things regularly enough, you'll eventually reach a point where the course of action you're following doesn't align all that closely to the real-life goals you would like to meet.

Failing to plan is planning to fail, and revisiting your strategy is critical to ensuring your long-term success and viability. What you'll need to do to succeed online years from now is likely to be a bit different from what you need to do now. And even if it wasn't, your company will have different goals and aims than the ones that are preoccupying you today.

## Going Back To The Drawing Board

As we wrap up these high-level thoughts on analytics and strategy reviews, I should mention that there is a final reason to monitor web stats very closely: because once in a while there's nothing to do but go back to the drawing board.

While it shouldn't ever happen to you if you're following the ideas in this book – which are ethical, tested, and proven – there are situations where Internet marketing plans fall completely flat. As a matter of fact, we tend to hear from business people who are at their wits' end on a fairly regular basis. Sometimes, it doesn't just seem like what they're doing isn't working, but that it's a waste of money and might actually be making things worse.

If you have any notion that you're in a similar situation, and it's been more than a few weeks since you put your new strategy in place, it might be better to stop everything and review your analytics before going any further. After all, the last thing you want to do is compound past errors, waste more money, and make things worse.

Even in the worst situations, there is hope. With good web analytics in place, you can assess what went wrong and make smarter decisions, based on better information, going forward.

There isn't any mistake you can't overcome in the world of Internet marketing, except for the blunder of not paying attention at all. Prioritize regular reviews of your web analytics and Internet marketing strategy, because they'll give you the fuel you need to keep your business firing on all cylinders.

# 10 | Find The Right Web Design And Internet Marketing Partner

Given what you've learned to this point, you could hire a company to design a great website for you and handle all the Internet marketing details yourself. But that wouldn't be my advice. Even when you work with websites, email, and social media accounts every day, as I do, there is still a lot to do and keep track of. Most business owners and managers have too much on their calendars already without the added burden of revising pages, double-checking SEO details, and coming up with new content ideas every week.

The analogy I often give to clients is that they should "be the driver, not the bus." In other words, it's important that you understand the *principles* of Internet marketing – the same ones I've outlined in this book – so you can choose the right team to work with, help shape strategy, and know what kinds of results you want.

When it comes to actually executing your plan, though, you might want to outsource some of the tasks to a web design partner... or at least have one that you are consulting with on a regular basis. Doing so can give you another perspective, and help you from making common blunders.

In this chapter, I'm going to show you what you should look for in a web design and Internet marketing partner, and then how you can make the most of their assistance…

## Finding The Right Web Design Team

Very often, the company you choose to handle your web design will be the same one that helps with your Internet marketing campaigns going forward, so it's important to choose carefully.

Most business owners pick a web designer by going to Google, clicking on a few local results, and then examining samples to see which ones they like. That's not a bad way to get the ball rolling, but it shouldn't be where your search ends and begins. In the same way that there is more to choosing the right spouse than going on mutual physical attraction, finding the right web design and Internet marketing team should involve more than a few shared artistic preferences. There's no sense in hiring a web designer if you don't like the look of the pages they produce, but don't stop there with your evaluations.

The right web design team for you has an aesthetic that you love *and* a few other important qualities. They should have a track record of success that you can verify, meaning that they haven't just launched websites for other companies like yours but have helped those businesses to increase their search visibility and become profitable online. They should be familiar with the kinds of challenges you are facing in your business, and be willing to learn about your industry.

In addition, any web design team you hire should have a working style that matches your needs. That means, at a minimum, that they are good listeners and communicators, and that they can adhere to the budgets and deadlines that you set. It also means that they treat you respectfully and put your preferences above their own artistic instincts when it matters.

These are all traits of a proven and experienced web design company, and the kind of details you can't necessarily get just from glancing at a portfolio. Remember, the real job of your creative team isn't to come up with a website that is pretty, but to impress your customers and make it easy for you to reach your real-world business goals. The best-looking website isn't going to do you any good if it costs too much, doesn't attract customers, or can't convert visitors into buyers.

## *The Real Key To Getting Great Creative Work*

Choosing a great web design and Internet marketing team is obviously crucial to your ongoing success, but to get the most from their knowledge and creativity, you're going to have to know how to work with them. In theory, this should be as simple as getting a proposal, writing a check, and waiting for the magic to happen. I can tell you from experience, however, that clients can make it easy or difficult for us to give them our best.

The first thing you have to know is that the most important work isn't done when we sit down to create layouts for your new website – it's when we learn about your business and the challenges or opportunities that are in front of you. Usually called "discovery," this step involves talking, questionnaires, and follow-up meetings.

A lot of new clients, eager to see their new website and start getting results, will try to rush through the discovery stage. They give quick responses and skip over follow-up questions, thinking that the answers must be obvious to everyone. Most companies come to a firm like ours because they want more sales, right? Shouldn't that be enough information to keep pushing forward?

It isn't. We need to know what current results are like, what kinds of customers you want to attract, who your biggest competitors are, what kind of personality you are trying to cultivate through your marketing, and so on. Take a little extra time and attention at the beginning of the design process to make sure everything is absolutely clear. We know you're anxious to get started, but clearing up misconceptions and misunderstandings in the beginning will save you huge amounts of time later.

Also know that once we get started, creating a website (and the subsequent Internet marketing plan) is a give-and-take process. One of the classic mistakes business people make is taking an "all or nothing" approach to contributing during the creative process. The most difficult clients are the ones that want to dictate everything, and not listen to any suggestions, or simply accept every idea we put forth without thinking it through.

Neither of these is helpful to your design and marketing team, and they could end up ruining your campaigns before they get moving. Remember that the job of your design partner is to take your insight and vision and turn it into something that works. If you don't take any of their advice – or worse, provide nothing in terms of solid direction – then there's a good chance the project will never get moving in the right direction.

And finally, try to be prompt and professional when providing feedback. Although we work with art, layouts, and web analytics all the time, we still can't read clients' minds. Saying that a design "has too much blue" is infinitely more helpful than giving the feedback that you "just don't like it." A good creative team will do everything they can to give you exactly what you want and need for your business, but you have to help them zero in on exactly what that might be at times by providing feedback.

## Delegate, But Don't Disappear

Once your new website actually goes live, lots of fun and exciting things can start to happen. This is the point where clients are usually most pleased and optimistic about what's to come. It's also the point when they realize that managing incoming leads and phone calls, online social accounts, blog posts, email newsletters, search advertising, and keyword strategies can get to be more than a little bit overwhelming.

Each of these is a static idea when your website is still in development. Once it has been launched, though, all of them have to be tended to in real time.

Know that it's perfectly acceptable if you don't want to manage every detail yourself. You can delegate certain tasks – either in-house, or to your web design and Internet marketing team – so long as you don't disappear. Ultimately, you can remain in control of your Internet marketing campaigns without typing every message or checking every keyword on your own. In fact, you'll probably see much better results if you stay hands-on in the areas that you excel at, and that matter the most to you, while letting someone else take the wheel on tasks that are technical or uninteresting.

To give a real-world example, a lot of business owners will maintain control of their own social media accounts, partly because they enjoy using sites like Facebook and Twitter, and partly because they feel it's important to maintain that one-on-one communication with customers and prospects.

At the same time, many of those same business owners and managers will delegate things like blog writing or search marketing management, because those tasks are time-consuming and tend to require professional skills (like writing ads and articles). They might give a bit of input when it comes to blog topics, or landing page themes, but leave the actual writing, designing, and posting to someone else.

That's a perfectly good solution, and it achieves a good balance of effort. It only works, however, if decision-makers at the company stay involved.

Things get a lot easier and more convenient when you simply sit down and write a check for your Internet marketing each month, but that's not really the best thing for your company. If you aren't an active participant in your own campaigns, you really won't know what's going on with them. And you certainly won't be able to tell why they are or aren't succeeding, and which directions you should pursue in the future.

In the same way that you should review your web analytics at regular intervals, and take a look at your online strategy to be sure it's working, it's important that you be in regular contact with your web design and Internet marketing team. How often depends a great deal on which kinds of activities you are pursuing, but if you aren't touching base at least once a month – and a few times a year to go over bigger ideas and make major decisions – then you probably aren't as involved as you should be.

## Working With A Web Design Partner Is All About Getting Results

Getting good web design and Internet marketing help does require you to dip into your budget, but also makes it possible for you to work smarter and achieve higher returns in the long run. As I told you in the beginning of this book, putting low-cost, high-ROI strategies to work isn't necessarily about spending as little money as possible, but getting the highest return from the investments you do make.

You could certainly argue that I'm biased in my view of the value that a good marketing partner provides. But I have also seen time and time again how easy it is for companies to go on the wrong track because they didn't have experience with a particular tool or idea. Pay-per-click advertising, for example, can be wonderful for increasing sales. However, it can also be used to burn thousands upon thousands of dollars in unprofitable clicks if you aren't careful.

As a business owner or executive, your job is to know what you need, not necessarily to look after every individual or technical task on your own. In the same way that lots of business owners know the basics of bookkeeping but still have an accountant and prepare their business taxes, the savviest marketers provide the motivation and insight needed to find new customers, even if they don't design every page or write every post themselves.

At this point in the book, you know what to do to make your Internet marketing campaigns efficient and successful. If you need a bit of help getting your plans off the ground, don't be afraid to benefit from a little bit of expert assistance. The results will be worth it!

# Conclusion:
## The Secret Sauce Isn't So Secret

Ready to take on the world? Going off experience, I know that a lot of you reading this book – especially if you took my advice and read it from start to finish the first time through – might be feeling some mixture of "excited" and "overwhelmed."

That's completely normal, and believe it or not it's a great thing. Because even if you feel like there's a lot to absorb right now, that's a sign that your mind is processing some new possibilities. Often, the hardest part about changing the results you get from online marketing is breaking free of old habits and thought patterns. By just reading this book, you have taken the first step in a better direction.

So how do you turn that enthusiasm into something you can use? You can begin by jotting down any ideas or inspirations that have come to you while reading through the chapters. Perhaps a couple of the concepts really stood out in your mind, and seemed especially pertinent to your company. If that's the case, act on those immediately.

Then, when you're ready, go back and look through the chapters again. Find the advice that seems most applicable to your situation, or the tips that seem to appeal most strongly to you. Or, move through the chapters in the order of their importance to your business. The point is that you should go back and take a look at each topic, one by one, so you can make the most of what you've read.

It's perfectly fine to do things at your own pace, and to start with the ideas that seem most likely to have an immediate impact on your business. While I firmly believe there is loads of great advice in this book, success (online or off) really comes down to taking what you've learned and applying it. I don't know exactly what's going on with your company, but you do. Take what you need and run with it.

More than anything, however, keep in mind that the secret sauce really isn't so secret. Or, to put things in a less riddle-like way, know that none of these chapters has the "one big thing" that makes a company really successful on the Internet. Instead, truly great things start to happen when they are all used together.

For example, a smarter approach to search engine marketing might save you a bit of money and bring you more targeted visitors. But when you combine that with buzz-building social networking strategies, a strong online reputation, and a user-friendly website, you have the makings of something that can have a significant impact on your bottom line.

Likewise, being smart about search engine optimization and local marketing can be a great way to introduce your business to thousands of new potential buyers, but integrating those new contacts into your email list and studying their behavior through analytics will make a much bigger difference than simply moving up a few places on Google's search engine rankings.

That's an important point to make for two reasons. First, I don't want you to become so focused on any one tactic or strategy that you ignore the others. It's an easy mistake to make, and it can end up holding you back from the kind of success you should be enjoying online. And second, the principles in this book are important, while specific tactics don't matter nearly as much.

To give you a sense of what I mean, let's go back to search engine marketing. The thought process behind narrowing your campaigns as tightly as possible, and matching your ads to both a type of person and a distinct landing page theme, is a proven way to boost results. It involves taking what's great about the web (individualized marketing) and opens up a world of possibilities.

At the same time, it doesn't really matter whether you are advertising through Google, Facebook, or some other pay-per-click platform. At some point in the future, Google might lose some of its popularity to a new search portal, or change its PPC system in a way that doesn't work as well for advertisers. So long as you are focused on the concept, and not the individual tool, you'll be just fine.

As long as you remember that the secret is in the approach to finding new customers, and not in technical details of web design or SEO, you'll always be prepared for the changes that are yet to come… and there are *always* changes in online marketing. It's the combination of effective strategies that works, even while specific tactics come and go.

With that, you have all the knowledge you need to go and build a profitable and spectacular online marketing campaign. Good luck, and don't forget to share your success story for future additions to this book or the accompanying website!

Paul J. Scott is the founder and president of GoingClear Interactive, a Boston-based web design and web development firm.

Entrepreneurial from a young age, Paul got his "big break" in the business world caddying for influential business leaders as a teenager in Nantucket. He carried the lessons learned from those encounters into the corporate world, where he got his professional start managing websites and advertising for a large publishing company.

In 2001, Paul decided to launch his own business, GoingClear Interactive, by working evenings and weekends in a shared studio space. A focus on creative thinking, client service, and commonsense solutions helped to grow the company quickly, and the firm is now considered a leader in custom web development. Today, GoingClear Interactive works with businesses, nonprofits, universities, and government agencies of all sizes, helping them to make the most of web programming and their websites.

A Boston native, Paul is a graduate of Bentley University and holds a master's certificate in web development and e-commerce from Clark University. When he's not finding new ways to make websites work, he enjoys spending time with his family, motorcycling, learning yoga, training in Krav Maga, volunteering for the Big Brothers program, golfing, and other activities.

You can learn more about Paul and his company GoingClear Interactive at GoingClear.com.

www.ingramcontent.com/pod-product-compliance
Lightning Source LLC
Chambersburg PA
CBHW050116210326
41519CB00015BA/3980